KANGAROO

Sandie Lee Books

Kangaroos

The kangaroos is a marsupial. It belongs to the family of 'Macropods.' Translated this means, "big foot." There are over 60 different species of kangaroos and their close relatives. The eastern gray kangaroo is the most common of them all. The kangaroo dates back millions of years. In fact, a fossil found shows one species may have stood 10 feet tall! In this article we are going to explore all things kangaroo, so let's jump right in.

Where in the World?

Did you know the kangaroo is only found in Australia? Depending on the type, this animal can live in open grasslands, in wooded areas, pastures, parks and even golf courses - they are highly adaptable. The kangaroo will stay where there is an abundance of food and few predators or threats.

The Body of a Kangaroo

Did you know the kangaroo comes in different colors? The fur of the kangaroo is soft and wholly. It can be grey to brown to red in color. The kangaroo has a long muzzle, wide set eyes and long ears that can be held straight up. Its tail is long and powerful and helps the kangaroo balance.

The Kangaroo's Feet

Did you know the kangaroo's back feet are super large? The front paws of the kangaroo are small and slender. Each one has 5 clawed digits on it. The back feet of the kangaroo are very strong and powerful. They allow the kangaroo to hop very quickly and are also used for kicking.

The Kangaroos Pouch

Did you know kangaroos have a pouch? The pouch is a large furry piece of skin located on the lower belly of the female kangaroo. This is used to house the baby kangaroo. Here the baby will nurse, grow and develop. The baby is always safe when it rides along in mom's pouch.

What a Kangaroo Eats

Did you know kangaroos are herbivores? This means they only eat plants. The kangaroo's diet consists of mainly grass, leaves, shoots and shrubs. Like a cow, the kangaroo regurgitates its food. This partially broken down food is brought back up and re-chewed, before it is swallowed again - like a cow does.

The Kangaroo's Special

Did you know kangaroos can box? When two male kangaroos are fighting, they will "punch" each other with their front legs. Kangaroos are also fast hoppers. They can reach speeds of up to 40 miles-per-hour. They can even jump 10 feet into the air and launch themselves 30 feet in one jump.

The Kangaroo as Prey

Did you know the kangaroo has few predators? African dogs called dingoes will hunt injured or old kangaroos. Man also poses a threat to these animals. The kangaroo is hunted for its fur, skin and meat. Kangaroo meat is eaten by people and made into pet food and the hides are made into shoes and other products.

The Kangaroo Territory

Did you know the kangaroo lives in a mob? Kangaroos are very social and like to live with other kangaroos. These gatherings are also called troops and can consist of up to 100 individual animals. Male kangaroos will fight other males for dominance (to be the top animal) among the mob.

Kangaroo Talk

Did you know kangaroos communicate through noise and sound? This animal will thump its powerful feet on the ground when it sees a predator coming. This alerts the mob to be on the look out. Kangaroos are also able to make hissing noises, coughing, clicking and grunting sounds. These are done when the kangaroo is angry, stressed and calm.

The Kangaroo Mom

Did you know the female kangaroo is called a doe or a Jill? Female kangaroos can get pregnant at various ages depending on the breed. A female kangaroo is always pregnant. As she is caring for her one baby in her pouch, she will have another baby in her tummy.

The Kangaroo Baby

Did you know the baby kangaroo is called a Joey? Baby kangaroos are born after only 36 days in their mother. They can be born the size of a grain of rice or the size of a honeybee. This little animal is blind and hairless, yet it still has to climb to its mother's pouch. Once inside it will nurse, grow and develop.

Life of a Kangaroo

Did you know the kangaroo can live to be only 6 years-old in the wild? Kangaroos not only fall prey to animals and humans, but droughts can lead this animal to starvation. In captivity, the kangaroo's life can be much longer - around 20 plus years. Here it is free from danger and fed a balanced diet.

The Eastern Gray Kangaroo

This is the most common type of kangaroo. The eastern gray can measure 10 feet from nose to tail and weigh around 145 pounds. It is grey in color with a lighter underside. It also has a very long tail. It measures almost 4 feet long! This kangaroo lives in the southern and eastern parts of Australia.

The Red Kangaroo

This type of kangaroo is the largest of them all. The males are reddish in color, while the females sport a grey colored fur. Males can weigh up to 190 pounds and stand about 5 feet tall. Females will be slightly smaller. It lives in large mobs on the dry, central areas of Australia.

Quiz

Question 1: What family does the kangaroo belong to?

Answer 1: The Macropods

Question 2: What is the main difference between the kangaroo's front feet and back feet?

Answer 2: The front feet are smaller with claws. The back feet are very long and powerful

Question 3: What can a kangaroo do that some humans do?

Answer 3: It can box

Question 4: How does a kangaroo alert other kangaroos to predators?

Answer 4: It will thump its feet on the ground

Question 5: What is a baby kangaroo called?

Answer 5: A Joey

Thank you for checking out another addition from Sandie Lee Books! Make sure to check out Amazon.com for many other great titles.

www.ingramcontent.com/pod-product-compliance
Lightning Source LLC
Chambersburg PA
CBHW040328010626
45792CB00024B/2285